Fulfillment by Amazon

Step-by-Step Instructions to Start a Fulfillment by Amazon Business.

© **Copyright 2016 by Bluecodex - All rights reserved.**

This document is presented with the desire to provide reliable, quality information about the topic in question and the facts discussed within. This Book is sold under the assumption that neither the publisher or the author should be asked to provide the services discussed within. If any discussion, professional or legal, is otherwise required a proper professional should be consulted.

The reproduction, duplication or transmission of any of the included information is considered illegal whether done in print or electronically. Creating a recorded copy or a secondary copy of this work is also prohibited unless the action of doing so is first cleared through the Publisher and condoned in writing. All rights reserved.

Any information contained in the following pages is considered accurate and truthful and that any liability through inattention or by any use or misuse of the topics discussed within falls solely on the reader. There are no cases in which the Publisher of this work can be held responsible or be asked to provide reparations for any loss of monetary gain or other damages which may be caused by following the presented information in any way shape or form.

The following information is presented purely for informative purposes and is therefore considered universal. The information presented within is done so without a contract or any other type of assurance as to its quality or validity.

Any trademarks which are used are done so without consent and any use of the same does not imply consent or permission was gained from the owner. Any trademarks or brands found within are purely used for clarification purposes and no owners are in anyway affiliated with this work.

Contents

Introduction 6

Foundations of FBA 9
    Create your Account 11
    Arbitrage 12

Amazon FBA Tools 15

How to Find Profitable Products to Sell 16
    Amazon Ranking System 16
    Amazon Guidelines 18
    Where to find items for your Inventory 18

Packing it Up: Shipping and Inventory Management 20
    Creating a Listing 21
    Labeling 23
    Creating a Shipment 24
    Packaging your Shipment 27
    Moving ahead with your shipment 29

Selling Fees 30
    Fee types 30
    FBA Revenue calculator 31
    Storage fees 32

Private Labeling with Amazon 34

Marketing **41**

    Your Sales Page 41

    Reviews Strategy and Getting Feedback from Buyers ... 42

    Amazon Advertisement Pay-Per-Click 43

    The Buy Box 48

How to Register a Business and Deal with Tax Issues **49**

    Federal Taxes 49

    Collecting Sales Tax 49

    Form 1040 52

    Business Registration 53

Wrap up: Amazon FBA overview **56**

Introduction

Everyone has heard of Amazon, but few people realize just how easy it can be to get in on the profits they reap. There are multiple ways to get involved with selling on Amazon, and this guide will provide step-by-step instructions on how to start your career as an Amazon FBA seller.

If you have ever considered a career as an entrepreneur, Amazon FBA is for you. Amazon has revolutionized the field of e-commerce, and there has never been a better time for you to take advantage of this growing industry. Using Amazon FBA, many vendors have gone from working a 9-5 job to taking charge of their own business and reaping profits larger than they ever earned working under someone else. There are numerous examples of sellers who have gone from inexperienced amateurs to six-figure moguls with the right approach to selling online.

Amazon is unlike other sales sites because it basically works as a search engine. Customers do not go to Amazon to browse. They are sure of what they want, and they know how to find it. Amazon is search-driven, which creates a unique relationship between buyers and sellers that makes it easy to break into for people with no previous sales experience.

The principle of FBA is simple, and works in a way similar to eBay. By finding products at huge discounts and selling them at a higher price through Amazon, you can earn a considerable profit. You will operate as a third-party seller on Amazon; when customers search for products on Amazon, you will notice that there are often other sellers whose prices are below Amazon prices.

As an Amazon FBA vendor, you essentially have your own business, but you operate under the protection of a large business and with access to the large customer base of the mammoth corporation that is Amazon. With the right marketing, you stand to make significant profit.

Fulfillment by Amazon works like this: you find the products and package them according to Amazon's stipulations. You then send them to an Amazon distributing center, the location of which is determined by the type of product you are selling. Amazon stores your products in one of its fulfillment centers, and your packages are sent off from there. Amazon essentially handles the front-end issues once you have taken care of the back.

What are the benefits of an FBA account over a regular individual seller account on Amazon? One of the benefits is that it can increase your productivity as a seller when you have more time in the day to focus on securing items to sell. When you are responsible for shipping your own products (as is the case with Merchant-Fulfilled sellers), you are responsible for packing and shipping everything yourself. There is only so much time in the day, so you are limited by your own productivity. With FBA, you can spend more time getting the deals you want and finding products to sell and less time with shipment.

Better still, you are offered the security of Amazon customer service. The items you sell, once they reach the Amazon warehouse, are under the responsibility of Amazon. This means Amazon handles customer service and returns, even packaging and delivery. Furthermore, your products can now be sold as Amazon Prime-eligible. This attracts customers who are more likely to purchase your items when eligible for free shipping and quick turnaround time. As a seller, you can rely on Amazon's sterling reputation for customer service to put you at an advantage over other sellers using the site.

It important to note that you as the seller do take responsibility for the product as it is sitting in the warehouse. The longer it is in storage, the more you will need to pay. So it is of critical importance that you choose the correct products that will sell quickly, and that you market them to your absolute advantage.

This book will tell you the tools, techniques, and tips necessary to maximize the potential of your small business. Follow these steps and you will be on your way to earning revenue sooner than you thought possible.

Foundations of FBA

Fulfillment by Amazon is all about strategizing; the difference between selling as a merchant and selling as a professional with FBA is the amount of time you will have to devote to maximizing your potential profit. Here are some basic guiding principles you will need to be aware of:

Buy Low, Sell High

This is how you earn money as an Amazon seller. There are multiple ways to do this; you can use the stores around you as a local resource for purchasing items cheaply. Depending on where you live, you may even be able to make money off of products that are not available elsewhere, and buyers are willing to pay big money simply for access. You may find yourself buying items at their normal price and selling them for a profit. This will be essential to running your business.

Competition

As an Amazon seller, your competition on the marketplace is huge. You must strive to be the best, most efficient seller you can be; this will lead to better reviews, which leads to higher listings. Amazon is a perfect platform for breeding competition among its vendors. It is set up in such a way to advantage the sellers who are already doing well.

This means to make the most of your business, you will need to run a tight ship, constantly checking to be sure you are offering the most competitive pricing. As you start off, you will need to focus on building credibility among your buyers and improving your reputation so you can move higher up in the ranks. There are strategies you can use to increase your visibility that will be addressed in this guide.

Technology

With Amazon FBA, you will be at your optimal productivity by using technology such as your cellphone to stay current with the top-trending products and to take advantage of the most complex apps on the market to calculate your best chances with selling.

Selling on Amazon FBA requires a level of dedication to working on a computer that those uncomfortable with the idea of adapting to new technology will be wary of. You will need to stay in tune and on top of the latest trends in online marketing if you wish to have a chance against the competition. This guide will direct you to some of the best resources on the market for getting the most out of your business.

What direction will this take you?

There are two ways to sell through Amazon FBA: through retail arbitrage, and with private labeling. People run immensely profitable businesses with both approaches, but they require different commitments.

Each form requires significant investment of time. With proper handling, you can turn your Amazon business into a full-time source of income. It doesn't happen overnight, however, and it takes time to build up the reputation and customer base to turn a sustained and secure source of income. This guide will equip you with the tools to understand the ways of the market, starting with the basics of Fulfillment and moving into the more complex routes, such as private labeling, toward the end.

Create your Account

First things first: you have to have an Amazon Seller account. If you are already selling on Amazon, you just need to register your account and "add FBA to your account." Otherwise, you will need an Amazon Seller Account. Sign up by scrolling to the links at the bottom of the Amazon homepage. Under the Header "Make Money with Us," click on the hyperlink that reads "Sell on Amazon." From there, you can register directly as an FBA seller, or start with your individual seller account.

Depending on what you sell, you may want to start with the individual seller before moving up to a professional seller account. There are advantages to starting with a professional seller account. Professional sellers are able to sell items that are restricted from individual sellers. Professional seller accounts are free for the first month, after which you can renew your subscription for a fee.

Individual sellers are sellers that ship less than 40 items per month. If you are planning to sell more than that, it is advisable to go for the professional account. There are differences in the fees you are charged as a seller depending on which account you use, which are explained in a later section. You can always upgrade from an individual account to a seller account – however, the opportunity for the first free month of selling professionally is only available when you first sign up. If you know you are serious about Amazon FBA as an investment in your future, go for the professional account and receive the first month free. You could always cancel it before the next month's charges set in.

All you need to sign up is your credit card information, name, address, a professional-sounding and snappy display name, and information to verify your identity.

In order to sell, you must complete a participation agreement that obligates you to fulfill Amazon's terms and conditions for selling. There are guidelines you will need to follow to be eligible to sell and restrictions on what you can and cannot sell. A partial list of guidelines is included in this guide, but be sure to check the Amazon official website for up-to-date information.

Now that you are registered to sell, you must figure out how you will acquire the products you will be shipping. There are many ways to do this, but this book will cover two main methods: arbitrage and private-labeling. Since arbitrage is the main way people usually get started, we will cover that method first for the foundations. Private labeling will be addressed in later sections.

Arbitrage

This is the word used to describe one of the fastest ways to get involved in Amazon FBA. There are multiple forms of arbitrage: be it through retail, garage sales, or online. It is the process of buying items at a discount or on clearance and selling them for a higher price through Amazon

Scanning and Scouting

Scanning and scouting is the most common way to begin your venture in retail arbitrage. Key to retail arbitrage are the apps you will use to scan your products and figure out the likelihood of selling off the items in the store. This business is not about taking chances; there are apps available for calculating the approximate profit you stand to make from selling such an item.

The Amazon Seller app is available for Android and iOS phones. Inventory Lab is another service that some recommend as it offers other tools for increasing your efficiency as well. Other scanning apps, such as Scoutify, Barcode Booty, and Profit Bandit, require a fee but come highly recommended.

In retail arbitrage, you scan the barcode on the product in the clearance aisle of the store. The app will display the information you need to determine how good of a deal it is and how much you are likely to earn selling that item. It calculates the profit for you. Depending on the app, you will also be asked to input the cost associated with your selling of the item – for example, the cost of the shipping materials you will need to send it to Amazon. This cost is one you will need to figure out over a period of time, because it is highly dependent on your personal circumstances.

You can repeat this process with retail items in any store, as well as with products of sale at discounts online and at garage sales. This can be done without an app, but it is easier to use your phone than to write the prices down and checking it at home. In the end, it is a personal preference, and trying both ways to see which is more efficient time-wise will not hurt.

The biggest issue people have with retail arbitrage is the amount of time that one must spend traveling from store to store. It requires a lot of energy. With proper scanning, however, it can pay off. It is generally wise to avoid items that are not less than 50% marked down in price. The best deals are on clearance for over 70% if you can manage it.

This type of arbitrage can be applied at yard sales or discount retailers, particularly with items like books. You will not necessarily be "scanning" if you look up pricing on items online, but the principle remains the same.

Scanning for the First Time

One way to feel comfortable and test out your Amazon FBA account is to scan products around your household that have not yet been removed from the packaging. This will give you an idea of how the apps work so you will be more comfortable when you are in an actual store scanning products. Furthermore, you can capitalize on the profitable opportunities you have lying around at home! Take a trip into the basement and make use of all those unwanted Christmas gifts. You may even go so far as to offer to help cleaning out your relatives' closets. You will be surprised at the rankings some products reach!

It is important to be aware of the restrictions on selling some products. Products with restrictions on them will be labeled as such on the scanning apps, but it is worth digging around the guidelines established by Amazon to know what you are getting into. A later section of this book addresses the very basics of what can and cannot be sold through Amazon, but for this type of information, it is best to go to the source.

Amazon FBA Tools

You will find in this guide that there are multiple services listed, from keyword finders to scanning systems, that will make your experience as an amazon FBA seller easier and more profitable. For almost any issue that troubles you, there are services available designed to make that task simpler. However, they can often be costly, and you may not have room in your margin to afford them. The easiest example is the scanning tools to help you find the most sellable products around. You'll read about some apps that have operating fees; the best one to start with though, is the Amazon Seller app.

One of the most important tools you will use is the FBA Revenue Calculator. As a beginner, the Amazon FBA Revenue Calculator is a free option to figure out what kind of profit you stand to make on an item based on the costs associated with it in comparison. You'll find more on this in the section on Selling Fees.

How to Find Profitable Products to Sell

The question of how to find profitable products to sell is one that depends heavily upon your preferred method of acquiring inventory. If you already have experience selling online and have the funds necessary to invest in your own line of products, head to the Private Labeling section for an in-depth description of the process.

If this is your first time venturing into online sales and you are looking for a quick easy way to get some experience selling and make a sizable supplementary profit, retail arbitrage is the name of the game.

After you've gotten comfortable using the scanner, it is time to hit the streets looking for those discounted and clearance items. The most important thing to address here is to find products for sale at a discount. At the same time, the product also needs to be able to sell. If it doesn't sell quickly enough, it will sit in the warehouses racking up fees. So, how do you know if an item will sell well?

Amazon Ranking System

Amazon uses its own raking system to categorize the products on its website. By looking at this ranking system, you can figure out how well an item sells. Items with lower numbers sell more quickly, which means more of them are bought on a daily basis. An item's ranking in included in the product description.

The Amazon Ranking System is important to understanding how the business of FBA works. First of all, know that a product's rank is based on its sales. It does not take into account reviews or ratings. This is not to say reviews and ratings are not useful; they can be encouraging for people to buy your items, which is how they ultimately contribute to the ranking a product earns. Sales are evaluated relative to other products in a category, so the ranking is not about the quantity of items sold.

Ranking plays an important role for all products sold on Amazon, but particularly for books, it becomes crucial to be aware of the item rank. If you are not selling books, it is important for different reasons. If you are looking at a product ranking for retail arbitrage, you are aiming for an item with a rank lower than 50,000 in its category. For private label, 12,000 is a better goal. The problem with sales rankings is that they cannot tell you everything about how an item will sell. They change over time and are based on the most recent sale period, so they are not necessarily reflective of an item's overall selling potential.

When you are looking to sell an item, you want to be sure that is desirable for the customer, but also that the competition is not too stiff to break into. To better get a sense of the accuracy of the sales rank, check out the reviews it has. If an item has many reviews and a good rank, you know that its rank is a result of sustained performance and not just a temporary jump.

If you are concerned about the rank of the product you are selling, refer to the section of this guide on Amazon Pay-Per-click (PPC) advertising, a sure-fire way to improve the visibility, and thus selling potential, of your product.

Amazon Guidelines

There are some products that cannot be sold through Amazon FBA. Counterfeit products are not allowed. You can check Amazon's restricted product list to figure out which items are disallowed by Amazon; some are not completely disallowed, but restrictions are placed upon them. A few examples from the list of restricted products include: alcohol, food and beverage, tobacco and drug paraphernalia, weaponry, make-up and skin care items, medical products, animals, electronics, services, and art. For a complete and up-to-date list with specific information on restrictions, it is advisable to visit Amazon's official website for more information.

If you are interested in getting approval for items that are restricted to sell on Amazon (for example, beauty products or foodstuffs), you will need to register with a professional account. Then, you will need to seek approval by submitting no less than 3 paper invoices from authorized wholesale suppliers in reasonable quantities (at least 200 units). Retail arbitrage will not work for getting approval to sell unauthorized products; you will need an established business.

Where to find items for your Inventory

Don't just limit yourself to the clearance section at Wal-Mart; there are tons of places to go to find deals for the savvy seller. Be aware of the characteristics that make an item ideal for selling on Amazon: cheap, in-demand, and easy to ship.

Retailers with steep discounts: Costco, Sam's Club, Dollar Tree and Dollar Family, Big Lots, Walgreens, CVS, Discount Books Stores (Libraries work in a similar way), Game Stop, Outlet Malls, toy stores, Marshalls, TJ Max.

Other resources: Yard sales, classifieds and Craigslist, estate sales

Packing it Up: Shipping and Inventory Management

Once you have the products you would like to sell in hand, you move on to the next stage: sending them to an Amazon Fulfillment Center. There are multiple steps to preparing your packages for further distribution that we will go through in the next sections.

With Amazon FBA, delivery of the product is under Amazon's responsibility. This means you are responsible for the packaging of the product in the first place. Amazon has strict guidelines and requirements for the products it delivers, so you must have the proper materials on hand in order to meet these requirements.

Often, Amazon requires you to ship the items you have bought to various locations, not just one. This is frustrating, but you must pay attention to the guidelines you are provided with. There are multiple reasons why your inventory may be split up. Often, it is because they will be sent to different locations so that customers can have access to them as soon as possible. This helps with faster shipping times to different parts of the country. Depending on what you are selling, you may also need to send it to a different location that is better equipped to handle or store special items.

In the last section we talked about the tools available through Amazon that help you find products to sell. There are other, more concrete tools you will need in order to sell through Amazon, as you will need to do the packaging of your products yourself. The following items will be absolutely necessary to your endeavors. Many of the products below you will be able to purchase through Amazon's Warehouse Network, which supplies Amazon-preferred products directly to its sellers.

- Computer

- Laser or thermal printer (Printer must be able to print scannable labels)

    o As your business expands, you may want to consider a Dymo label printer to quicken the process of printing

- Labels

- Boxes that adhere to Amazon regulations

- Packaging materials

- Appropriate place bags depending upon product type

- Measuring tape

- Shipping tape

- Scale for measuring weight

- Smartphone

- Price-tag peelers (for retail arbitrage)

Creating a Listing

Once you have figured out a product to sell, you have to make the listing available for viewing on Amazon. To do this, you must add items to you inventory. On your Amazon Seller account page, click on the "Inventory" tab. Then click "Add product." Clicking "Add Product" will prompt you to enter a search term for the item you wish to sell. You can search with any number of identifying factors, such as the barcode or the product name. It is not necessary to add a new product, unless you are selling something you have made yourself.

When you find the product you wish to sell, you will be prompted to fill out the product information, which includes important factors, such as the price you are selling your item at, the condition of the item you are selling, and how you will ship the item.

When describing the condition of the item, choose your words carefully. As with the importance of detail with listing the item, the more vivid your description, the better your repertoire of trust you build with potential buyers. While you are only required to enter "Acceptable" or "good," it is better to give the buyer a better idea of the condition so they can make a more informed decision (and compared to those items with no description, yours will generally seem better by virtue of attention to detail.)

At the same time, you want to be truthful in your description. If you lie about the condition of the item, you are only setting yourself up for poor reviews.

When you are selecting the shipment method, choose the following option: "I want Amazon to ship and provide customer service for my items if they sell" to indicate that you will be using the FBA service.

Selecting FBA

After selecting the option for Amazon to handle delivery and customer service, there is one more necessary step. Under

"Inventory," select "Manage Inventory." Click on the drop-down menu labeled "Actions" and select "Change to Fulfilled by Amazon".

Labeling

Amazon's shipping and receiving is reliant upon barcodes. Everything you send to Amazon has to have the proper label so they know they belong to your account. They help with being able to track the items during the shipping process. The Amazon labels can be printed from within your Amazon seller account.

After selecting the action to Fulfilled by Amazon, you will be prompted to choose, if you wish, from two labeling preferences.

FBA Labeling Service

You can pay extra to have Amazon do the labeling of your inventory for you. Calculate your own labeling costs; it may be worth it, particularly if you spend a lot of time labeling your products, to use Amazon's labeling service.

If you are selling under a private label, you may find it cost-efficient to send Amazon's labels to your manufacturer so they send the products directly to Amazon. This could be an option, depending on your manufacturer. Instead of paying freight costs to you, labeling the items, and sending them to Amazon, you may be able to save freight costs and pay for only one journey straight from the manufacturer to the Fulfillment center.

Some products can be sent using the manufacturer's barcode, but you should consult the Amazon website for more information on this process. If you are using the labeling service, you save yourself the time of having to affix Amazon labels to them. However, there still needs to be some identifying factor, such as a barcode, that packers will use to determine how to properly label it. The following codes are eligible to suffice as barcodes: UPC (Universal Product Code), EAN (International/European Article Number), ISBN (International Standard Book Number), JAN (Japanese Article Number), or GTIN (Global Trade Item Number).

Stickerless, commingling inventory

Stickerless commingling inventory means less work for you. It is only available for products that are new; it means that your inventory will be added to that of other sellers who are selling the same thing. When someone buys the item you are trying to sell, Amazon may take from the inventory of another seller whose items are stored in a Fulfillment Center closer than the one your items are stored in. This works to the advantage of Amazon by enabling them to ship an item quicker and provide more optimal customer service. This also means other peoples' items could sell before yours; it ends up being a grab bag. Many sellers advise against this option, saying that the extra work when it comes to labeling is worth it in terms of the profits. Furthermore, only certain items are actually eligible for commingling.

Creating a Shipment

1. Log into your Seller account and head to the Manage Inventory sections under the Inventory header. On Manage Inventory, click on the items you plan to ship and select Send/Replenish Inventory.

2. Once there, choose the options to create a new shipping plan.

3. Enter the information about the items you are shipping, where you are shipping from, how many products you are shipping, and whether or not there may be restrictions on the items you are submitting for shipment.

4. Review the Prepare Products section to understand the preparation that is required of you to send your products to the Amazon warehouse. More about these requirements is elaborated upon in the Packaging section of this chapter.

   a. If you would like Amazon to handle the preparation of your packages (this entails a fee), choose "Amazon" from the Who preps drop-down menu. Otherwise, as the merchant, you will be responsible for preparation. Some products are not eligible for preparation by Amazon.

5. For labeling your products, you will need to know whether you would like to do commingling, stickerless inventory or affix the labels yourself.

6. With this information filled in, you can now print your labels for affixing to the products from either the Label products page or the Manage Inventory page.

7. After labeling, you will be brought to the Preview shipments page. This is where you will find out if your inventory has been split up into multiple shipments.

8. To finish up your shipment, select "work on shipment."

9. Now you will need to determine how to ship your goods to Amazon. This depends on whether you will do small parcel

delivery (SPD) or less-than-truckload shipping (LTL). This distinction is generally made based on the size of the shipments. For shipments over 150 pounds, you will opt for LTL, though this is no longer set in stone as a rule, and you may find a better deal with your particular carrier.

a. You must have decided on a product carrier in order to complete this section. You should choose a carrier that is convenient for you to access and that has good pricing on the items you are shipping. Costs can vary depending on where you are asked to ship the inventory. Using an Amazon-partnered carrier can save you the work of tracking each package on your own. For SPDs, UPS is the only partnered carrier at the time of publication.

b. Once you've entered the number of boxes you will be shipping, you can print your labels.

Printing your Amazon labels

When you create a shipment through your Amazon seller account, you have to print Amazon barcodes. The labels are what make it possible for the funds to go to your account. Amazon requires that you label each item, unless you sign up for the commingling service. For the purpose of earning the highest margins possible, we will not discuss the commingling service in depth in this guide. Your labels must be readable and scannable, which is why Amazon stipulates a laser or thermal printer should be used rather than an inkjet printer, because inkjet printers bleed.

When affixing a label, the original product label should be covered by the FBA label to avoid confusion. Each and every item you ship requires an individual label. There are different sizing requirements for the labels you use and you should be able to print the labels without tampering with the sizing using editing software. Amazon Labels have the following information on them:

FNSKU: stands for Fulfillment Network Stock Keeping Unit – This code is included on the product label so that the scanners are able to associate the unit with your account, meaning the correct item is pulled for the sale. The units you sell have an FNSKU code that is individual to your account, so if your products get mixed up in the handling, scanners can trace the ownership of the item to you so it doesn't get lost. It is also related to the specific Amazon Standard Identification Number (ASIN), which is assigned to every product sold on Amazon.

The labels also include the name of the product and the condition that the product is in as identified by you, the seller.

Packaging your Shipment

You need to package your items so they are able to be sent properly from Amazon once they reach the warehouse. You will be charged a fee if they are not properly packed. You will have to account for the personal costs of packaging materials when calculating the revenue. Amazon has strict regulations. Be sure to take into account the costs of the packaging materials when you are selecting an item.

Fragile items: Must be packed in bubble wrap so they can be dropped without breaking.

Liquids: Must be packed in a sealed bag with a suffocation warning.

Clothing and other cloth items: Must be packed in a sealed bag with a suffocation warning.

Toys and children's products: Must be packed in a sealed bag with a suffocation warning.

Small-grain or powdered materials: Must be packed in a sealed bag with a suffocation warning.

Sold in a set as one unit: Must be packed in shrink wrap and placed in a bag or box with a sticker indicating a complete set is there.

Packaging can be handled by Amazon if your products are marked with a UPC (Universal Product Code.) There is a fee associated with this as well.

There are very specific requirements for shipping that go beyond what goes inside the box. You must also pay careful consideration to the size of the box, which cannot be more than 25 inches on any side. There are specific weight requirements as well. Refer to amazon's Shipping and Routing Requirements regularly to ensure you are up-to-date on shipping requirements. Items that do not meet the requirements are refused and may be returned to you, usually at your cost.

Once your labels are affixed, your items properly packaged in compliance with the regulations, and you know which carrier is responsible for your items, it is time to send them off! Schedule a pick-up with your carrier or drop it off at the nearby facility. In line with the Amazon FBA service, your physical work is done once the items have reached the warehouse. (The work you are responsible for now takes place virtually in the form of marketing the items you have sent off.) However, there is more to it than that.

Moving ahead with your shipment

Once you've sent your shipment, you must be sure they all arrived on time. The View Summary page of your shipping plan provides information about whether or not anything is missing from your shipment. If there is something missing from your shipment, you can request an investigation and Amazon services will inform you of the potential cause for the discrepancy.

If something is lost, damaged, or missing, you will be informed of this and will need to consult Amazon for further action with regard to reimbursement (if it wasn't your fault) or the fees you will be charged with upon return shipping (if the issue was from your end.)

Selling Fees

As you are sending your items off, be aware of the fees you will incur using the FBA service. Amazon does take a portion of the revenue you generate, but in the grand scheme of things, it usually pays to have this minor bit taken out. FBA fulfillment fees are constantly changing; you will need to keep a vigilant watch of the prices to notice how they fluctuate, usually around the time of the change in financial quarter.

Multi-Channel Fulfillment

The fees you are charged for using the FBA service depends on whether you are using only Amazon Fulfillment or Multi-Channel Fulfillment. Multi-channel fulfillment applies to sellers who are using other venues to sell their products, for example using an Etsy page or their own website. Sellers using Multi-Channel use Amazon as one way of directing traffic flow to their other selling channels. If you are interested in Multi-Channel fulfillment, you can look into this option for your business.

Fee types

Fees are applied to your items based on handling of the order, Pick and Pack, and the weight handling. This is why lightweight items can be particularly advantageous for your business. Fees are also applied differently for Media, Non-Media, and Oversized items. Non-Media items are classified in size tiers and also product type.

If you are selling an item over $300.00 worth in cost, you are able to sell it at no cost in terms of the fees leveraged against it.

FBA Revenue calculator

To learn more and calculate the fees that will be leveraged against your items, Amazon has made the FBA Revenue calculator available to its sellers. You need the following information to calculate the revenue you have the potential to earn on an item.

Item Price – what you plan to charge for the item.

Shipping – Because you are shipping through Amazon, they are taking over the fees, so this cost is assumed to be $0.

Order handling – this is determined by the type of item you are shipping and whether or not a flat rate exists for it.

Pick and pack – refers to the cost of the packaging materials necessary to ship your item to the warehouse. You will need to look at materials requirements established by Amazon for packing, which differ depending on the type of item. If you do not properly pack your items, you will be charged for this once they arrive at the warehouse.

Outbound shipping – with Amazon FBA, this is calculated as a flat rate depending upon the item.

Weight handling – Calculated using the scale specified by Amazon, with a special fee included for certain items, such as TVs.

Monthly storage – Charged by cubic feet of volume, differs monthly.

Inbound shipping – the cost of transporting your items to the Fulfillment center. If the items you are ordering have proper labeling, they can sometimes be sent directly to Amazon. This applies specifically to private label goods. With private label goods, your manufacturer can send the items directly to an Amazon warehouse if they meet Amazon requirements. Otherwise, you are responsible for shipping the goods.

Customer service – With FBA, the cost of customer service is already factored into your professional seller account, so there is no charge here.

Prep service – This applies if you opt for Amazon to fulfill your item prep and it is calculated per item.

Once you have inputted the above values, the Revenue Calculator will tell you the Referral cost and the Variable closing fee.

Storage fees

Amazon charges sellers a fee for storage, which is why it is critical to select items that sell well and quickly. Otherwise, you will be charged for the items that remain in storage. You are charged for the total cubic feet of your items.

The cost of the charge per cubic feet of your items varies depending on the time of year. Storage is more expensive in the latter half of the year due to the demands of the holiday shopping season. If your items sell slowly and are in storage for over 6 months or a year, depending on the item, you will be charged a long-term fee. This does not apply to single items; rather, the long-term storage fee only applies to items in bulk.

Before you get discouraged about the costs of shipping and handling, know that there is a key difference here between individual selling plans and professional selling plans. With an individual selling plan, an extra $0.99 is levied against the cost of your item in exchange for the FBA service. Professional selling plans allow you as the seller to keep that $0.99, preserving and strengthening your profit margin.

To avoid storage fees, keep the dates of inventory clean-up in mind. Amazon goes through its inventory on August 15th and February 15th; so as you are planning on dates to restock, consider how close you are to running into one of those dates.

Private Labeling with Amazon

Private labeling differs from retail arbitrage; it is the process of buying from a supplier and reselling these items under your own private brand. Retail arbitrage is good for starting out, but you may find yourself desiring more. Arbitrage can be limiting because of the amount of time you must spend, often physically, in transporting yourself from store to store and checking out pricing. With private labeling, you spend less time on the hunt for new inventory. Private labeling is for serious sellers only; this is the big league.

Private labeling requires that you launch your own product line. It is not recommended to jump into private labeling cold: you will need to build up the product line first. You would have a hard time making any sales from scratch, because you would not have any traffic to work with to generate sales. You need good reviews and a solid sales base to move your listings up in the rankings in order to make any sales.

Unlike retail arbitrage, which requires daily searching for a source of income, private labeling can ease the process significantly because you no longer have to spend all of that time searching for products in person. Furthermore, your supply can always increase in quantity if it sells well in a way that is impossible with retail arbitrage.

Find a Product to Sell

Just like with retail arbitrage, you will need to devote time to locating the perfect product. This is all about finding your niche. You need to find a product that is in-demand, but with a market that is not over-saturated with competitors. This is a lesson that can be applied to your search for arbitrage goods as well, but becomes even more important in the quantities of inventory that you will be handling with a private label. The perfect place to do this is the best-seller rankings. Amazon does this for the buyer's benefit, but it is easy to see how this can be used to the advantage of the seller.

Best-seller rankings do the hard work for you; it is an informal version of market research. It tells you what the customers are already buying, instead of forcing you to run the risk of testing a product only to see that it doesn't sell. Since you already know what is selling well, you are saving yourself money and energy by using it as a resource.

Depending on what you'd like to sell, check the top 11 best–sellers for that category. If you have no preference, just look through all of the categories. There are characteristics that lend themselves naturally to great selling options: things that rank well, do not weigh a lot, and are not typically associated with a brand.

Low-weight items are ideal because your shipping costs are lower. But brand name items? Remember, you are selling your own brand. It is not possible for you to sell Adidas shoes, for example, because those products are protected under patents and cannot be sold under your private label.

The purpose of private labeling is to create your own brand, under your name. This is why you should be selecting products that are easy to sell under your moniker. Cooking products or office supplies are good examples, provided they are made with lightweight materials.

Who else is selling it?

After finding a product you're interested in, you should look into how the other guys are doing. You are selling the same product as other people in the business, so you need to study them and learn their strengths and weaknesses to be able to refine your own strategy.

In the following hypothetical example, we'll be talking about an apple corer. What else do you need to know about apple corers, besides that they sell well, in order to be a successful seller? You'll need to see how the other guys are doing it. Search for your product in Amazon's search engine.

Get systematic about it: take notes on the first few listings that come up to compare pricing, the number of reviews, and information about the appearance of the listing itself. A quality listing is evident; you yourself should be aware of the elements of an attractive, professional and informative listing, so scout out the ones you are competing against for the same qualities you would expect of yourself.

When you take a look at your notes, there are things you should be looking for. It should take you a while to find a product that fits these categories. Don't be surprised if a few hours go by. This kind of research is time-consuming, but it does pay off in the long run. The time you spend searching is time you will have saved by using FBA instead of doing the delivery and customer service on your own.

 You want a price that is high enough to earn you reasonable profit, but low enough to be within the average consumer's range of affordability: the lowest you would want to see is $8, and the highest $45. The other things you are looking for have to do with making the competition easier for you to scale. A low number of reviews is something to aim for, because it means you will need fewer reviews to come up in the search results. In a similar vein, look for products in which most of the best-sellers rank at less than 1,000. The less stiff the competition, the better. Poor quality or just average-looking listings are a further aspiration for the same reason.

So, let's say you've found that apple corers meet the all the requirements of this category and move forward.

Contact and Negotiate with a Supplier

Now you're looking for someone who can supply you with apple corers. The most cost-effective options are international suppliers; it is rare to get anything comparably inexpensive that is manufactured in the US. Alibaba is the database of choice for most FBA sellers; it is an international market place with thousands of listings for the products you are interested in selling.

Search for your product on Alibaba and find the product you are looking for. Be wise and do your research on the suppliers.

In private labeling, you are looking for a product that sells at a 3x multiplier for what you originally paid for it. If you buy something for a dollar, you should be able to sell it for at least 3 dollars. When you find a product that is profitable, ranks well, and fits the guidelines as dictated by Amazon regulations, you should be ready to reach out to the supplier.

When reading the listings, you are looking for information about what is necessary to place an order. Most suppliers have what is called a minimum order quantity (MOQ), which is how many units of the item you will need to purchase. They may also include information on the lead time, which is the amount of time it takes for them to deliver the product to you. It is not guaranteed that they allow for private labeling, so be sure to check that as well.

Even with this information readily available in the listing, you will need to contact the supplier personally. This is actually to your advantage as a buyer, because before you get started, you'll want to order a test batch so you can examine the quality of the product for yourself. Negotiate with the suppliers on the price of these test orders; smart manufacturers are eager to make new business connections, and so they will be more willing to give you a decent price on this test order. It is possible to negotiate with a supplier and reduce their MOQ to 300 or 200 units, which eases the burden on you to sell them off if you are less than impressed with the product itself.

Establish your own brand

While you are searching for the perfect supplier and product, you should be crafting your private label brand. This seems intimidating; after all, you may not have any marketing experience at all, and are suddenly expected to design your own campaign.

Thankfully, there are professionals out there willing to take on the task of doing the design work for you. You do not need to go it alone. Sites such as Fiverr and Upwork put you in contact with design professionals who will take care of the branding for you.

Some sites function so that you are the one to reach out to the designers with your project, whereas others have designers bid on your project proposal. The service you want to use depends on how much work and funding you want to put into design.

Superior design is what will set your product apart from others who are selling the same product. Work on a snappy name and streamlined design that entices buyers. In online shopping, this is one of your most powerful selling points.

When the design is finished, get the files to your supplier so they can carry out the order you've made.

Crafting your listing

While you are waiting for your order to come in, spend time refining the product listing. You should follow the same guidelines established above for products gained through retail arbitrage. Be sure to include a vivid product description; often, sellers don't put any effort at all into writing a description, but their products still sell well. Imagine the potential of your product when paired with an excellent description.

The first sale

Your first sale is always the most difficult to make. Without a credible reputation and trusted base of customers, you have little to work with when marketing your product. Word-of-mouth cannot be overrated as a technique; building your base is essential. This works with private labeling in the same way it can work with retail arbitrage, and is covered more thoroughly in the marketing section of this guide. There are techniques you can employ on your own page, services you can use internally with Amazon and external methods as well. The time that you do not spend searching for inventory can now be used to enhance your marketing skills.

Private labeling and earnings

Private labeling requires some initial investments funds, unlike retail arbitrage. The profits you stand to make, however, are often considerably more significant. With products that do exceptionally well, by ranking in the top 100 of their category, sellers can reap thousands in revenue on a daily basis. Items that rank in the top 500 have the potential of earning you a few hundred dollars a day. Even products in lesser rankings can result in a steady flow of side income.

There is no right or wrong amount to spend getting your product off the ground. You may only wish to spend a few hundred, or you might want to go big with a few thousand. If you are confident in your profit margin, the opportunities await you.

Marketing

Amazon functions essentially as a search engine, and it is your job as a seller to improve your sales so your products show up earlier in the results. There are many strategies available to sellers for improving visibility, and you will have to experiment to find the ones that work for you.

For example, you can offer multiple shipping options on your product by editing your Shipping Settings. This is helpful, for example, if you are selling a product that often requires replacing. With this option, buyers will consistently be signed up to receive your product. This obligates you to keep a steady stock of the product so as not to disappoint your buyers and risk bad reviews.

Your Sales Page

Customers interface with your business through a sales page. Your sales page is the first thing customers interact with in your business, so you should make sure it is professional in appearance and accurately represents the quality of the products you are selling

Think carefully about the name you select to represent your business to others – be sure it is legible and professional-sounding.

Use broad keyword in descriptions for your items so they are more likely to come up in a search, but be careful not to cram the product title with too many descriptors – buyers are wary of spam and can recognize a ploy. One tool you can use for figuring out the best keywords for your products is the Amazon Keyword Tool, which utilizes Amazon's Autocomplete search tool to show the most popular keywords used on Amazon. When people type in a word on Amazon, its engines use real words searched by its buyers to suggest search terms for completion. If you are using keywords that show up in the Autocomplete results, your product is more likely to come up in the buyer's search. Keyword Tool Dominator is a service you can use to emulate the results of the Autocomplete service employed by Amazon.

Do not underestimate the value of quality bullet point descriptions. Customers use the descriptions to make decisions between products. Many of the products you sell may be similar in price and appearance to other products from different vendors. Your item descriptions are your chance to shine. The more helpful they are, the better trust you build with potential buyers. They are not, however, the place to make false promises. Be sure the information you provide in the item descriptions is vivid yet factual, honest, and truthful.

Appearance is everything. You won't be relying on your cellphone camera to take picture of your products. Some sellers outsource the task of editing photos to make them professional grade.

Reviews Strategy and Getting Feedback from Buyers

Good reviews are essential to successfully running your business. Unfortunately, 90% of Amazon buyers do not leave reviews after purchasing a product. It is important to reach out to people to get good reviews – you must build customer trust in order to expand your reach. The easiest way to do this is to provide incentives for customers to leave reviews for your products. In your position as a seller, you are able to offer your customers a special promotional code for when they are buying your products.

Offer them a discount, sometimes even a free product, in exchange for leaving a review. This does require that you put some of your money on the line, but in the context of your overall operating costs, it is highly worth it. This can help you makes sales and get reviews – the kinds of activities which in turn lead to higher listings and even more business. By lowering the buyer's perceived sense of risk with a low price, they will feel more inclined to take the chance on a new company.

A quick online search will show any number of coupon companies seeking to offer verified coupons for Amazon products. You can submit your promo codes through these sites for your products and watch your activity flourish from there.

Amazon Advertisement Pay-Per-Click

There are internal ways to advertise through Amazon that you should be aware of as a seller to make the most of your business. The primary way that people make purchases on Amazon is through their searches. Most searches are what we call "long-tail searches," meaning that people tend to search three words or more to get the best and most accurate results. Considering how many products are for sale on Amazon, this makes sense. Millions of searches are made on Amazon each month.

As previously mentioned, buyers on Amazon are unlike buyers from other companies. They know exactly what they want. Their searches are thus very powerful. When a buyer searches for something on Amazon's search engine, the most relevant products to their search are brought up. There are two kinds of results displayed when a customer makes a search: organic results and paid results. Organic results are items from sellers with good ratings and reviews. Paid results are displayed even before the organic results.

To make the most of paid results, you have to know the basics. It is not just submitting your listing; rather, you must understand the keywords that work behind it.

Your first Campaign

Amazon makes it easy to create a campaign internally. You will use Amazon Services to make your product into a Sponsored product. You manage advertisement using the Advertising section located in Seller Central. Ads are organized into campaigns so you can measure the effectiveness of your advertising.

Start by creating a new campaign. Choose an easy name you can alter in the future for different campaigns. The name remains visible only to you, so it needs to make sense to you. You will be asked to input further values about your campaign. When it comes to the budget, it is a personal preference, but many sellers recommend beginning at $50-$80 a day. This number indicates the maximum of what you would be spending per day, rather than the actual price of the campaign. It is unusual to reach the maximum cost anyway, and as a beginner, you can spread your net wide. Afterward, you will be able to adjust to a more exact value.

You may be wondering how much you should spend on advertising. Like with many options you will be faced with as the owner of a small business, this answer is dependent upon personal preference. Based on the margin available to you and what you see as a worthwhile investment in the long term, how effective your previous attempts at advertising have panned out, all of these factors contribute to your decision. If you're making money, though, and turning a profit, there is no wrong answer. Spend as much as you find profitable. The bottom line may seem intimidating at first, but seeing in the context of spending per-unit rather than on an overall budget can help you better understand the whole benefit of your advertising.

Calculating the Average Cost of Sale, otherwise known as the ACOS, will help you determine how much sense it makes to spend on advertising for a single product. To calculate the ACOS, determine the following:

Your established Selling Price

Cost of Goods Sold (the price you paid to acquire what you are selling)

All FBA Fees (Based on storage, etc.)

Miscellaneous variable costs (cost of shipping, packaging, etc.)

Using the Apple Corer as an example-

Selling Price: $27

Cost of Goods: $4

All FBA Fees: $11

Miscellaneous: $3 (this is just the shipping cost from the Chinese supplier to the Amazon warehouse).

By subtracting the COGS, FBA fees, and Miscellaneous from the Selling Price, we are left with $9 in profit per unit. This leaves up to $9 available from a sale to still make a profit.

Next, you're looking to find the ACOS threshold to find the break-even point. To do this, split the net income from the selling price. Using the figures above, we end up with a 33% ACOS threshold. This translates into profit on using any advertising with a Cost of Sale at 33% or less.

With knowledge of how much you can spend, you can be more informed about what kind of campaign makes sense to pursue. There are two kinds of campaigns you can start with: automatic and manual. With automatic targeting, Amazon establishes the search words that will bring up your ad, whereas in manual, the choice is yours.

Automatic targeting campaigns could not be easier: all you have to do is select and enable under "Create a campaign."

Manual Campaign Creation

Manual campaigns require a bit more strategy. With a manual campaign, you upload you own list of words. Finding the words is where it becomes tricky: how do you know what words will make you the most successful?

There are plenty of websites and services the scour data on customer searches to find out what people are most likely to search. You could use sites such as Ahrefs, or keywordtool.io. Google Keyword Planner is a free service once you create an account with AdWords.

(You can use Google AdWords to direct traffic to your listing through Google Searches. AdWords cost money, but if there is room in your margin, it may be a worthwhile option to consider)

Keyword planners are easy to use: in the search bar, type some general description words that you apply to your product. The Keyword site will list words that are similar and show you the monthly volume for those words.

Use these tools to generate the best keywords to find your product, those that have the highest monthly searches.

Then, you will add them to your campaign. Select the product you would like to advertise. Then, paste the keywords you found on the search sites into the box underneath the suggested keywords.

How many keywords will you want to use? There is no magic number; depending on your budget, you may want to prioritize quality over quantity. Veteran sellers suggest 100 in your manual campaign to start, and you can add or subtract from there, in addition to the words suggested by the automatic campaign. While that may sound like a lot, think of the long-tailed searches; there is no telling what could come up. Using the data from the week after your campaign runs will help you decide which words are worth keeping.

It's that easy! Now that your campaign is running, it is tempting to keep a close eye. It will take up to 3 days for Amazon to run the metrics on the data, so don't be alarmed if you aren't seeing results right away. It is important not to make changes to you campaign at first, at least for a week's time. Otherwise, you won't be able to make meaningful observations about the data. After a week has passed on your campaign, you will be able to make true observations about its quality.

With impressions and clicks, there is potential for phishing and false clicks. Amazon will sort through and determine which ones were legitimate and which ones were not, which is why the processing takes some time.

Filter your data with metrics to figure out where you are spending money and whether or not investing in certain search terms is to your benefit. Some of the most useful terms to filter by are Keyword by ACOS, Spend, Broad Match, and Bid.

How and when you run your campaigns is up to you. Some say to wait until you have at least 10 reviews. It can also help to start before that, though, because PPC campaigns will usually help raise the ranking of your product by virtue of simply being more popular, and the earlier you start with them, the sooner you can start analyzing data.

The Buy Box

The "Buy Box" is the ultimate goal for your product. When a customer is buying a product through Amazon and multiple vendors are selling the same new product, the buyer has the option of selection from one of those vendors rather than the Amazon product (though there are restrictions on the ability to sell books, movies, music and DVDs in the Buy Box). This is one of the best ways to reach buyers, because it puts your product right in their faces. The Buy Box is not an option that can be bought; it must be won. To do this, you have to have excellent records with competitive pricing and consistent availability.

How to Register a Business and Deal with Tax Issues

Many people do not realize that signing up as a FBA seller on Amazon has implications for business and taxes. For this reason, you will most likely need to register your business in order to collect tax from the buyer on the items you sell and pass those taxes on to the state. Amazon works on a quarterly system, so you will need to collect your tax information on a quarterly basis.

Federal Taxes

Your business constitutes a form of self-employment. For this reason, you will need to do the paperwork for the Self-Employment tax in order to pay for your income tax. You will also need to pay Medicare tax on your salaried income and Social Security taxes, though this depends on the income you make.

Collecting Sales Tax

The first thing you will need to do is register with the sales tax board of the state you are living in. Only after doing this can you begin to collect taxes on the items you sell. Otherwise, you will be collecting taxes illegally.

If you are already a seller on Amazon, you will be familiar with the obligation to collect sales tax. However, while in many ways, Amazon FBA makes running your business easier in terms of tax collection, it becomes a little more complicated.

This is because you are utilizing Amazon's distribution warehouses in multiple states. You are thus involved in multiple state tax nexuses. The legal situation surrounding nexuses is still in limbo – there are new developments happening all the time. Because online businesses are so new, regulations regarding sales tax are still in their infancy and you will need to be vigilant about these issues to be sure you are in compliance with the most up-to-date versions of these laws.

There are only 5 states that do not collect sales tax in the U.S. Every other state has one form or another of requirements about collecting sales tax. If your inventory is being stored in a state, you will need to collect sales tax on it. As an individual seller, this is pretty straightforward: you are shipping from your home state, and will need to register your business there and get a permit to collect sales tax there.

With FBA as a professional seller, it is not so straightforward. This means you need to find out where Amazon is storing your inventory. Once you find out where the merchandise has been stored, then you can go about registering for permits to collect sales tax on the items you have sold.

Since you are running a small business, there are tax tips for calculating your overall spending. When buying items through retail arbitrage, save the receipts. Be sure to record the mileage of your trips to the store as business expenses.

It is advisable to get into contact with a tax accountant to avoid running into legal issues once your business becomes profitable. This guide will help with the basic outlines of the action you can take with regard to initial awareness of tax issues, but it is not comprehensive.

Where should I be collecting sales tax?

You will find this information in your Amazon reports. Access your Reports on the Seller Central page. Under the Inventory tab, click on "Inventory Event Detail" and download the report. Once you have loaded the report into Excel (or whatever spreadsheet reading software you choose to use), you have to find the specific column that tells you where your items have been shipped.

Use the filter tool to look up the column with the name fulfillment-cent-id. This is the name used in Amazon reports to show where your goods have been stored. It consists of a three-letter code followed by either a 1, 2, or 3. The letters indicate the code for the airport closest to the distribution center. So the airport is usually located in the state of the distribution center. By looking up the airport codes listed in your Amazon report to find out what state they are located in, and comparing those airport codes to the locations of Amazon Fulfillment centers, you should be able to tell which states your items have been stored in.

There are also services available that will find this type of information for you if you are inclined to outsource this work.

How do I collect taxes in the states I have a sales nexus in?

Once you have established the locations of the states where your goods have been stored, you will likely need to apply for a sales tax permit or license for that state.

Each state has different requirements for registering for a sales tax permit. You will need to apply and register for every state your items are stored in. Most states do not charge a fee for registering as a business and collecting sales tax, which is not to say that all of them don't. There are five states that do not require any registration.

Tax Collection Services

You can pay for a service that will establish your tax needs for you and take care of the rest. There are other websites with guides on the requirements for registering in every state that also offer services for handling your taxes through Amazon, however, it is wise to consult a lawyer to avoid making mistakes and risk auditing.

Amazon also offers its own services for Professional Sellers. By clicking on the "Settings" section of Seller Central, you can select "Tax Settings" and begin setting up Amazon's tax collection services. Amazon charges for its tax collection services, but it may be worth the charge in light of the extensive complications brought up in dealing with so many tax nexuses. With Amazon's service, you are required to calculate the refunds yourself.

Form 1040

As a small business making over $400 dollars in profit, you are required to file Form 1040. A general rule of thumb for this type of tax on your income is that 30% of what you earn must be set aside for taxes. It may seem like a lot, and it varies from business to business, but that is a reasonable figure to expect. This is because you are no longer paying income tax (assuming your Amazon FBA business has become your main source of income).

To find out the income you've earned on your business, you will use the Data Range Reports for a detailed report that offers a record of your income as well as of your expenses.

The important thing to keep in mind with taxation is that you keep a detailed record of your income and expenses. If you want to deduct the costs of running your business (for example, transportation to and from the shipping center, or to retail locations, and the supplies you use to operate your business) then you need receipts. The more costs you are able to deduct, the lesser your income will appear, and the lower the taxes you will need to pay.

Business Registration

With Amazon FBA, you are your own small business. There is often a question of whether or not you should register your business legally. Whether or not you need a business license to operate is a matter of state law. Many states only require licensing for stores with physical locations. Depending on what you are selling, you may need liability insurance. As a business owner, it is generally advisable to have insurance on your property.

When you are starting out, it is a good idea to formally register your business for tax-collecting purposes. Also, it adds a level of protection. For example, if someone were to counterfeit your items, you would have the legal standing to go after them. If someone were to sue you for a faulty product, you would also have protection to rely on. This also means that if you needed to take out a loan for any reason, you would be able to do it as a business. There are a few options here that this guide will outline. It is important to consider taxes and the form of business you will have in order to avoid the risk of auditing from the Internal Revenue Service (IRS).

Register your name

In order to register a business, you will need to have a Doing Business As name (DBA). This is a fictitious business name that is needed for any business if you do not want to name it your personal name. It is needed for sole proprietorships and Limited Liability Companies. To register, you need to go to either the county clerk's office or through the state government, which depends upon the state you live in.

With a DBA, you can pursue other types of business ownership.

As a Sole Proprietor business, you are afforded low overhead costs, but you take on the risk of legal infractions alone. If someone ever had reason to sue from your project, you would be responsible personally and your wealth and property would be on the line.

Should you choose to start a Limited Liability Company (LLC), would be protected from some of the claims that could be leveraged against you as the Sole Proprietor. For that, however, you would pay different taxes. With a single-member LLC, you may be treated the same legally as a sole proprietor entity. If, however, you are going into a multiple-partner LLC, you would be subject to different taxes. There is a lot of variation with regard to these entities, so check the local laws of your state.

If you are interested in registering as a corporation or under a trade name, speaking with a lawyer trained in the law regarding Amazon FBA would be to your advantage. You can always start out as a sole proprietor and switch business entities later on down the line.

Taxpayer Identification Number

A Taxpayer Identification Number is not a business license, but it is used by the IRS when doing taxes with your business. Even though your social security number would suffice, it is advisable to get a TIN because wholesale companies (for your private labeling endeavor) are more inclined to treat you seriously which is advantageous when it comes to negotiation over inventory.

Wrap up: Amazon FBA overview

After reading through this guide, you should feel informed and ready to get started embarking on the journey of FBA business ownership. The benefits are obvious and the potential for profit is enormous if you are willing to put in the strategic work and effort. Many people have invested the time and turned Amazon into their main source of income – now you can too.

It starts off simply: creating your account and arming yourself with the tools of the trade. With the right apps, you can figure out the best way to get a bang for your buck. You'll become an expert at the practice of buying low and selling high, especially with the help of the tools that software developers are continually improving.

Once you've built up your inventory of items you sought out with expertise for their appropriate ranking and adherence to Amazon restrictions and guidelines, you are ready to start a shipment. The packing materials are costly, but remember that you will be able to deduct the cost from your income at the end of the tax season. When you create a shipment with your Amazon Seller account, you will receive detailed instructions on how to pack your shipment and where to send it.

When you've sent your first shipment, be aware of the selling and storage fees that will be levied against you. The advantages of being a professional seller are numerous, but particularly with regard to these selling fees, since you won't pay extra for every item. Use the FBA revenue calculator, another tool in your toolbox, to determine the potential earnings from your sale.

If you feel comfortable with retail arbitrage but are seeking to take it to the next level, or if you are entering Amazon FBA with previous experience selling online, private labeling is for you. Buying inventory cheaply and marketing it under your personal brand is a way to ramp up your earnings. The competition is fierce, but if you choose your products wisely, it can have huge rewards. Even with the right product choice, you will still need to do the most to market your business and get the coveted Buy Box benefits.

A lot of marketing is just common sense: you need to have an attractive sales page so your products present well. There are tricks of the trade, however, that will improve your standing. Offering discounts can help get you the necessary exposure to generate reviews, and taking advantage of Amazon's advertising function with the help of keyword-finding aids will improve your chances – as long as you know how to properly invest in your campaigns.

The technical side of things can get complicated, but this guide should help you feel more comfortable in the awareness of the potential pitfalls that lie ahead. Amazon businesses are rewarding, but you need to be properly equipped with the right legal knowledge in order to avoid the consequences of a mismanaged business.

Once you get started with Amazon FBA, you may find yourself encountering unique issues that aren't addressed in this guide. For those situations, you can address your inquiry to the online community of the FBA Sellers through Seller Central or on other communities like Reddit. There forums offer a framework for the exchange of novel ideas that could revolutionize your selling. Be open to the suggestions of others, as they could help you get ahead of the game.

Lastly, never fail to remember the importance of investing in yourself, for yourself. With Amazon FBA, you are in control. This means you have to be capable of motivating yourself to make the most of this opportunity. The more work you are willing to put into FBA, the more you will get out of it, but only if you are willing to go the distance. It may be called passive income, but you have to actively strive to reach that point. The time you don't spend going after your share of the market is time you leave to other people to take it from you. After reading this book, the next step is to go register as an FBA seller. Armed with this knowledge, the success is yours for the taking.

If you have enjoyed this book, I'd greatly appreciate if you could leave an honest review on Amazon.

Reviews are very important to us authors, and it only takes a minute to post.

Thank you

Printed in Great Britain
by Amazon